GREAT QUOTES
from GREAT
Women

From **Marie Curie** to **Michelle Obama**—inspiring
words from women who have shaped our world

Peggy Anderson

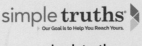

simpletruths.com

Dedicated to my mother, Mary Crisorio, whose unconditional love and support have been my greatest inspiration.

—Peggy Anderson

Introduction

Great women are not considered so because of their personal achievements but for their abilities to speak out on behalf of the lives of countless others. To boldly face diversity and discrimination, yet continue to show daring feats of bravery in spite of the obstacles before them. They speak with both a compassionate heart and great strength of character. They are true leaders who have advanced not just womanhood but the world around them.

We hope reading the words of these great women will inspire all of us—our mothers, daughters, our sisters, even our future granddaughters—to embrace our own greatness. For once we can revel in the power of our own voice, we too can speak out for what is right and impact the world for the better.

Contents

Christiane Amanpour

I HAVE ALWAYS THOUGHT IT MORALLY UNACCEPTABLE TO KILL STORIES, NOT TO RUN STORIES, THAT PEOPLE HAVE RISKED THEIR LIVES TO GET.

One of today's leading news correspondents, Christiane Amanpour is a British-Iranian journalist and television host. She is the Chief International Correspondent for CNN and hosts CNN International's nightly interview program *Amanpour*. Additionally, Amanpour is the Global Affairs Anchor of ABC News and has worked for *60 Minutes*.

Amanpour was born in London but spent time in Iran before going to boarding school in England at the age of eleven. Things changed for Amanpour in 1979 when the Shah of Iran was overthrown by a revolution, as this event sent her family into exile but also ignited her interest in journalism.

Throughout her career, Amanpour earned multiple journalistic awards, such as multiple Emmys and Peabodys and an Edward R. Murrow Award, along with recognition from the Library of American Broadcasting.

We in the press, **by our power**, can actually undermine leadership.

If we have no

respect for our viewers,

then how can we have

any respect for ourselves

and what we do?

What we do and say
and show *really matters*.

❦

No matter what the hocus-pocus focus

groups tell you, time has proven that

all the gimmicks and all the cheap

journalism can only carry us so far.

Maya Angelou

I'VE LEARNED THAT MAKING A "LIVING" IS NOT THE SAME THING AS MAKING A "LIFE."

Maya Angelou overcame a troubled childhood to become a noted poet, writer, and activist. Her first job was that of the first black female streetcar conductor. This was the first in a series of extraordinary achievements.

Early on, Angelou fine-tuned her natural dancing and acting talent to eventually earn a dance scholarship. Her performance career included a European dance tour and a plethora of television shows and records. After holding a position in the Southern Christian Leadership Conference, she moved to Egypt to edit a weekly newspaper. Two years later, Angelou became an administrator and instructor at a Ghana music school. Twice nominated for a Pulitzer Prize, Angelou also wrote an autobiographical novel series to cope with the grief she felt after Martin Luther King Jr.'s assassination on her birthday.

Through her varied experiences on life's journey, Maya Angelou is the embodiment of the American Renaissance woman.

Courage is the most important of all the virtues, because *without courage* you can't practice any other virtue consistently. You can practice any virtue erratically, but *nothing* consistently without courage.

I've learned that people will forget what you said, people will forget what you did, but people will never forget *how you made them feel.*

You may not control all the events that happen to you, but *you can decide* not to be reduced by them.

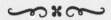

I have found that among its other benefits, *giving liberates the soul* of the giver.

I don't personally trust any revolution where *love* is not allowed.

See, you don't have
to think about doing
the right thing.
If you're for
the right thing,
then you do it
without thinking.

The most called-upon prerequisite
of a friend is an accessible ear.

I've learned that you shouldn't go
through life with a catcher's mitt on both
hands; you need to be able
to throw something back.

How important it is for us to recognize
and celebrate our heroes and she-roes!

Susan B. Anthony

CAUTIOUS, CAREFUL
PEOPLE, ALWAYS CASTING
ABOUT TO PRESERVE
THEIR REPUTATION…
NEVER CAN BRING
ABOUT A REFORM.

Susan B. Anthony is best remembered as a pioneer and crusader of the women's suffrage movement in the United States. President of the National American Woman Suffrage Association, her work helped pave the way for the Nineteenth Amendment to the Constitution, giving women the right to vote.

Discouraged by the limited role women were allowed in the established temperance movement, Anthony helped form the Woman's State Temperance Society in New York, one of the first organizations of its kind. She devoted herself with vigorous determination to the abolition movement, serving from

1856 to the outbreak of the war in 1861 as an agent for the American Anti-Slavery Society.

Attending the International Council of Women in 1888 and the International Woman Suffrage Alliance in 1904, Susan B. Anthony was a major catalyst for social change in America and abroad.

Failure is *impossible*.

Men, their rights, and

nothing more;

women, their rights, and

nothing less.

The day will come when men will recognize woman *as his peer*, not only at the fireside, but in *councils of the nation*. Then, and not until then, *will there be the perfect comradeship*, the ideal union between the sexes that shall result in the highest development of the race.

Mother Teresa

I SEE GOD IN EVERY
HUMAN BEING. WHEN I
WASH THE LEPER'S WOUNDS
I FEEL I AM NURSING THE
LORD HIMSELF.

Mother Teresa, born Agnes Gonxha Bojaxhiu, is revered for her lifelong dedication to the poor, most notably the destitute masses of India.

In 1928, at the age of eighteen, she went to Ireland to join the Loreto Convent in Rathfarnam, Dublin, and shortly thereafter traveled to India to work with the poor of Calcutta. In 1950, after studying nursing, she moved into the slums of the city and founded the Order of the Missionaries of Charity. Mother Teresa was summoned to Rome in 1968 to found a home for the needy, and three years later, she was awarded the first Pope John XXIII Peace Prize. By the late 1970s, the Missionaries of Charity numbered more than a thousand nuns who operated sixty centers in Calcutta and over two hundred centers worldwide.

Mother Teresa's selfless commitment to helping the poor saved the lives of nearly 8,000 people in Calcutta alone. Her compassion and devotion to the destitute earned her the Nobel Peace Prize in 1979. Following her death, Mother Teresa was beatified by Pope John Paul II.

We shall never know how much *good* a simple smile can do.

The **hunger for love** is much more difficult to remove than the hunger for bread.

Don't look for big things, just
do small things with great love.

❧ ✳ ❧

Loneliness and the feeling of being

unwanted is the most terrible poverty.

Humility is the mother of all virtues; purity, charity, and obedience.

❧✳❧

Let no one ever come to you without leaving *better and happier.*

❧✳❧

Now let us do something *beautiful* for God.

We ourselves feel that what we are doing is just a *drop in the ocean*. But if that drop was not in the ocean, I think the ocean would be less because of that missing drop.

❧✲❧

Do not allow yourself to be disheartened by any failure as long as you have *done your best*.

Marie Curie

AFTER ALL, SCIENCE
IS ESSENTIALLY
INTERNATIONAL, AND IT IS
ONLY THROUGH LACK OF
THE HISTORICAL SENSE THAT
NATIONAL QUALITIES HAVE
BEEN ATTRIBUTED TO IT.

Polish-born French physicist Marie Curie was famous for her work on radioactivity. From childhood, she was remarkable for her prodigious memory and intellect.

One of Curie's outstanding achievements was understanding the need to accumulate intense radioactive sources, not only for the treatment of illness, but also to maintain an abundant supply for research in nuclear physics. She is the first to have realized that radioactivity was an atomic quality, and she even coined the term. Her insights paved the way for other researchers to discover the neutron and artificial radioactivity. Shortly after this discovery, however, Marie Curie died from leukemia caused by the radiation.

Twice a winner of the Nobel Prize, Marie Curie made immense contributions to physics, influencing subsequent generations of nuclear physicists and chemists.

In science, we must be *interested in things,* not in persons.

Be less curious about people and more curious about ideas.

I was taught that the way of progress was neither swift nor easy.

Life is not easy for any of us. But what of that? We must have perseverance and above all confidence in ourselves. We must *believe* that we are *gifted* for something, and that this thing, at whatever cost, *must be obtained.*

You cannot hope to build a **better world** without improving the individuals. To that end, each of us must work for his own improvement, and at the same time share a general responsibility for **all humanity,** our particular duty being to aid those to whom we think we can be most useful.

I am among those who think that science has *great beauty*. A scientist in his laboratory is not only a technician: he is also a child placed before natural phenomena which impress him like a *fairy tale*.

Melinda Gates

WOMEN AND GIRLS
SHOULD BE ABLE TO
DETERMINE THEIR OWN
FUTURE, NO MATTER
WHERE THEY'RE BORN.

Encouraged by her mother to pursue an education, Gates became interested in computers during an advanced math class in grammar school, which led her to pursue computer science at Duke University. In 1987, she began working for Microsoft where she worked on projects like the website Expedia.

In 1994, Gates and her husband (creator of Microsoft) started a foundation that initially meant to give computers and Microsoft products to libraries all over the country. Today, Gates has expanded this foundation to address issues like global poverty and health. A powerful American businesswoman and philanthropist, Gates's primary focus is now how to make our world a safe, renewable resource for everyone.

If you want to see things happen at a global level, *start at the village level.* Give women the tools and education and they will drive the change.

Sometimes it's
the people you can't
help who inspire
you the most.

I'm wholehearted about whatever I do.

❖

If you are successful, it is because somewhere, sometime, someone gave you a life or an idea that started you in the right direction. Remember also that you are indebted to life until you help some less fortunate person, just as you were helped.

❖

All lives have an equal value.

Ruth Bader Ginsburg is the Associate Justice of the Supreme Court of the United States, which makes her the second female justice in the country's history. Encouraged by her mother to embrace education, Ginsburg enrolled at Harvard Law School as one of nine females in a class size of approximately 500 students. She transferred to Columbia Law School after her husband took a job in New York City, becoming the first woman to be on two major law reviews—the *Columbia Law Review* and the *Harvard Law Review*.

Ginsburg's start to her legal career was not ideal; being a mother to a young child, a wife, and Jewish at a dangerous time in our history, she struggled to find a job. Eventually, Ginsburg became an associate director of the Columbia Law School Project on International Procedure and spent time in Sweden where she began to develop more insight on gender equality. Back in the States, Ginsburg became a professor at Rutgers Law School and was one of fewer than twenty female professors in the country. Here she cofounded the first U.S. law journal about women's rights—the *Women's Rights Law Reporter*.

Ginsburg has devoted most of her career to fighting for women's rights as a constitutional principle. In 1972, she cofounded the Women's Rights Project at the American Civil Liberties Union, and between 1973 and 1976, she argued six gender discrimination cases before the Supreme Court and won five of them. In 2009, *Forbes* named her among the 100 Most Powerful Women, and in 2015, *Time* included her as one of the Time 100.

I think **our system** is being polluted by money.

The side that wants to take the choice away from women and give it to the state, they're fighting a losing battle. *Time is on the side of change.*

We should not be held back from *pursuing our full talents,* from contributing what we could *contribute to the society,* because we fit into a certain mold—because we belong to a group that historically has been the object of discrimination.

People ask me sometimes, "When will there be enough women on the court?" And my answer is: "When there are nine."

If you have a caring life partner, you help the other person when that person needs it. I had a life partner who thought my work was as important as his, and I think that made all the difference for me.

Every now and then it helps to be a little deaf...

That advice has stood me in good stead. Not simply in dealing with my marriage, but in dealing with my colleagues.

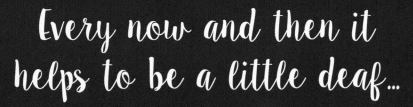

Jane Goodall

LASTING CHANGE IS A SERIES OF COMPROMISES. AND COMPROMISE IS ALRIGHT, AS LONG YOUR VALUES DON'T CHANGE.

Known for her fifty-five-year study of chimpanzees in Tanzania, Jane Goodall is a British primatologist, anthropologist, and animal rights activist. Born in London, Goodall was interested in animal behavior from a very early age and engulfed herself in literature on zoology and ethology.

Goodall's interests in animals eventually led her to Lake Tanganyika in the Gombe Stream Reserve where she sought to observe the social and family interactions of wild chimpanzees. After multiple attempts and years of watching the chimpanzees, Goodall became a familiar presence to the primates who were no longer threatened by her. Her discoveries have led to new understandings of primates but also to new perspectives on protecting the environment.

In 1977, Goodall founded the Jane Goodall Institute, which focuses on conservation and development programs in Africa. A similar program, Roots & Shoots, was created over a decade later to help educate the youth and promote positive changes to the environment.

The most *important* thing is to *actually think* about what you do.

What you do makes

a difference, and

you have to decide

what kind of difference

you want to make.

The greatest *danger* to
our future is *apathy*.

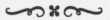

Every individual matters.
Every individual has a role
to play. Every individual
makes a difference.

Change happens by *listening* and then *starting a dialogue* with the people who are doing something you don't believe is right.

We have the choice to *use the gift* of our life to make *the world a better place*— or not to bother.

❧✖❧

Only if we understand, *can we care*. Only if we care, *we will help*. Only if we help, *we shall be saved*.

Audrey Hepburn

TAKING CARE OF CHILDREN HAS NOTHING TO DO WITH POLITICS. I THINK PERHAPS WITH TIME, INSTEAD OF THERE BEING A POLITICIZATION OF HUMANITARIAN AID, THERE WILL BE A HUMANIZATION OF POLITICS.

As a film and fashion icon of the twentieth century, Audrey Hepburn demonstrated staunch humanitarian beliefs throughout her life.

Born in Belgium, she grew up with a passion for ballet and the stage, making her debut in the London theater. Coming to America at the age of twenty-two, Hepburn made her mark on the film industry by making thirty-one films and ultimately receiving five Academy Awards.

Her most notable work, however, was off screen. She spent much of her time and energy working with UNICEF to provide assistance to disadvantaged families in multiple developing nations. As Goodwill Ambassador for UNICEF, Hepburn brought to the attention of the world the need for food, immunizations, and safe water in underprivileged countries. Her efforts garnered her several awards, including the Presidential Medal of Freedom. Audrey Hepburn remains a legendary Hollywood humanitarian.

The best thing to **hold onto**
in life is **each other**.

I was born with an enormous *need for affection,* and a terrible *need to give it.*

For beautiful eyes, *look for the good in others*; for beautiful lips, *speak only words of kindness*; and for poise, walk with the knowledge that *you are never alone*.

THE "THIRD WORLD"

IS A TERM I DON'T LIKE VERY

MUCH, BECAUSE WE'RE

ALL ONE WORLD.

Living is like tearing through a museum. Not until later do you really start absorbing what you saw, thinking about it, looking it up in a book, and remembering—because you can't take it all in at once.

Arianna Huffington

IF YOU TAKE CARE OF
YOUR MIND, YOU TAKE
CARE OF THE WORLD.

Cofounder and editor-in-chief of the *Huffington Post*, Arianna Huffington is a Greek-American author, syndicated columnist, and businesswoman. She studied economics at the University of Cambridge where she became president of the Cambridge Union—the university's noted debate organization.

With a strong interest in politics, Huffington ran for governor of California but later withdrew. She chose a different way to interact with the world by founding the blog the *Huffington Post*, which covers topics such as politics, business, entertainment, environment, technology, lifestyle, women's interests, and local news. The blog became a major hit and was acquired by AOL, designating Huffington as the editor-in-chief of the Huffington Post Media Group.

Treat people like family, and they will **be loyal** and give their all.

A purpose of human life, no matter who is controlling it, is to love whoever is around to be loved.

We need to accept that we won't always make the right decisions, that we'll screw up royally sometimes—understanding that failure is not the opposite of success, it's part of success.

Fearlessness is like a muscle. I know from my own life that the more I exercise it the more natural it becomes to not let my fears run me.

KEEP YOUR FACE TO
THE SUNSHINE AND
YOU CANNOT SEE
THE SHADOWS.

Helen Adams Keller was born in Tuscumbia, Alabama, in 1880. A severe illness in infancy left her deprived of sight, hearing, and the ability to speak. Her life represents one of the most extraordinary examples of a person who was able to transcend her physical handicaps—accomplishing more with her impairments than many do in their lifetimes.

Through the constant and patient instruction of Anne Sullivan, Helen Keller not only learned to read, write, and speak, but went on to graduate cum laude from Radcliffe College in 1904. In addition to writing several articles, books, and biographies and cofounding the American Civil Liberties Union, she was active on the staffs of the American Foundation for the Blind and the American Foundation for the Overseas Blind. She also lectured in over twenty-five countries and received several awards of great distinction.

Helen Keller's courage, faith, and optimism in the face of such overwhelming disabilities had a profound effect on all she touched. Her tremendous accomplishments stand as a symbol of human potential.

Life is either a *great adventure* or nothing.

Alone we can do so little;

*together we can
do so much.*

Security is mostly a superstition. It does not exist in nature, nor do the children of men as a whole experience it. Avoiding danger is no safer in the long run than outright exposure. *Life* is either a ***daring adventure*** or ***nothing***.

The Bible gives me a deep,

comforting sense that

"things seen are temporal,

and things unseen

are eternal."

Happiness cannot come from without. It must *come from within*. It is not what we see and touch or that which others do for us which makes us happy; it is that which we think and feel and do, first for *the other fellow* and *then for ourselves.*

Loretta Lynch

EVERYONE WANTS TO BE SEEN. EVERYONE WANTS TO BE HEARD. EVERYONE WANTS TO BE RECOGNIZED AS THE PERSON THAT THEY ARE AND NOT A STEREOTYPE OR AN IMAGE.

Loretta Lynch was the eighty-third U.S. Attorney General and the first African American woman to hold this position. She was born in North Carolina into a family that participated in the Civil Rights Movement. After graduating from Harvard Law School, she worked as a litigator in New York until 1990 when she started working as a prosecutor for the U.S. Attorney team of New York's Eastern District, which launched her career in government.

Lynch has worked on high-profile cases such as those involving police brutality, corrupted lawmakers, and money laundering by Fédération Internationale de Football Association top officials.

Our most effective response to *terror* and to hatred is compassion, it's unity, and it's *love*.

A LICENSE TO

PRACTICE LAW IS NOT

A LICENSE TO

VIOLATE IT.

The power to arrest—to deprive a citizen of liberty—must be used fairly, responsibly, and without bias.

Others will always seek to define you based on what they think you represent or who they think you are. But you have to be the one to control what you do and what you say and how you present yourself.

Margaret Mead

NEVER DOUBT THAT A SMALL GROUP OF THOUGHTFUL, COMMITTED CITIZENS CAN CHANGE THE WORLD. INDEED, IT IS THE ONLY THING THAT EVER HAS.

American anthropologist Margaret Mead's great fame owed as much to the force of her personality and outspokenness as it did to the quality of her scientific work.

As an anthropologist, she was best known for her studies of the nonliterate peoples of Oceania, especially with regard to various aspects of psychology and culture, the cultural conditioning of sexual behavior, natural character, and culture change. As a celebrity, she was widely known for her forays into such far-ranging topics as women's rights, childbearing, sexual morality, nuclear proliferation, race relations, drug abuse, population control, environmental pollution, and world hunger.

Elected to the presidency of the American Association for the Advancement of Science at the age of seventy-two, Margaret Mead held twenty-eight honorary doctorates and a posthumous Presidential Medal of Freedom. All achievements to be proud of but none more than the life she dedicated to an understanding of the origins and continuing development of humanity.

We are living beyond our means. As a people we have developed a lifestyle that is draining the earth of its *priceless* and *irreplaceable* resources without regard for the future of our children and people all around the world.

If we are to achieve a richer culture, rich in contrasting values, we must *recognize* the whole gamut of *human potentialities*, and so weave a less arbitrary social fabric, one in which each *diverse human gift* will find a fitting place.

A society which is clamoring for choice,

which is filled with many articulate groups,

each urging its own brand of salvation,

its own variety of economic philosophy,

will give each new generation no peace

until all have chosen or gone under,

unable to bear the conditions of choice.

The stress is in our civilization.

Golda Meir

THOSE WHO DON'T
KNOW HOW TO WEEP
WITH THEIR WHOLE
HEART DON'T KNOW
HOW TO LAUGH EITHER.

Golda Meir was a founder of the State of Israel and served as its fourth prime minister. Born in Kiev, Ukraine, she immigrated to Wisconsin in 1906. Her political activity began as a leader in the Milwaukee Labor Zionist Party.

After immigrating to Palestine in 1921, she held key posts in the Jewish Agency and in the World Zionist Organization. After Israel proclaimed its independence in 1948, she served as minister of labor, and then foreign minister. Meir was appointed prime minister in 1969.

During her administration, she worked for a peace settlement in the Middle East using diplomatic means.

However, these efforts were interrupted by the outbreak of the fourth Arab-Israeli war. She resigned her post in 1974 but remained an important political figure throughout her retirement.

Golda Meir's true strength and spirit were emphasized when, after her death in 1978, it was revealed that she had suffered from leukemia for twelve years.

Don't be **humble**, you
aren't that great.

I never did anything alone. Whatever was accomplished in this country was accomplished collectively.

YOU COULD CERTAINLY
SAY THAT I'VE NEVER
UNDERESTIMATED MYSELF,
THERE'S NOTHING WRONG
WITH BEING AMBITIOUS.

Best known as the first female chancellor of Germany, Angela Merkel is a politician and one of the creators of the European Union. Although she originally was a physicist and chemist, Merkel decided to get involved with politics after the fall of the Berlin Wall in 1989. After joining the Christian Democratic Union (CDU), she was appointed as Minister for Women and Youth and later as Minister for the Environment and Nuclear Safety. Almost a decade after being elected Secretary-General of the CDU, Merkel was appointed Chancellor of Germany in 2005.

Some of Merkel's greatest accomplishments are maintaining a blossoming economy, shutting down nuclear reactors in search for alternative energy sources, and helping in the negotiation of the Treaty of Lisbon and the Berlin Declaration.

There is nothing worse
than **sweeping** a threat under
the mat and just living
from day to day.

A good compromise
is one where
everybody makes
a contribution.

It seems to me that the fact that I am a woman is a bigger issue than the fact that I'm from the East. For me it isn't really important. I've only ever known myself as a woman.

Without freedom the human mind is prevented from unleashing its creative force. But what is also clear is that this freedom does not stand alone. It is freedom in responsibility and freedom to exercise responsibility.

WERE THERE NONE WHO
WERE DISCONTENTED
WITH WHAT THEY HAVE,
THE WORLD WOULD NEVER
REACH ANYTHING BETTER.

An English nurse, Florence Nightingale was the founder of trained nursing for women.

While in charge of nursing at a Turkish military hospital during the Crimean War (1854–1856), she coped with overcrowding, poor sanitation, and a shortage of basic medical supplies. As Nightingale made her nightly hospital rounds, she gave comfort and advice, establishing the image of "The Lady with the Lamp" among the wounded.

Regarded as an expert on public hospitals, she was dedicated to improving the health and living conditions of the British soldier. In 1860, she founded the Nightingale Home and Training School for Nurses, the first such school of its kind in the world.

Florence Nightingale has been immortalized as the epitome of tender care.

How very *little* can be done

under the spirit of fear.

I attribute my success to this—

I never gave or
took any excuse.

I never lose an opportunity of urging a practical beginning, however small, for it is *wonderful* how often in such matters the mustard-seed germinates and roots itself.

I can stand out the war with any man.
I stand at the altar of the murdered men, and, while I live, *I fight their cause*.

Michelle Obama

WE LEARNED ABOUT
DIGNITY AND DECENCY—
THAT HOW HARD YOU WORK
MATTERS MORE THAN HOW
MUCH YOU MAKE… THAT
HELPING OTHERS MEANS
MORE THAN JUST GETTING
AHEAD YOURSELF.

Born in Chicago, Illinois, on a cold day in January 1964, Michelle Obama has gone from sharing a one-bedroom apartment with her parents and older brother to living in the White House as the forty-fourth first lady of the United States. A graduate of Princeton and Harvard Law, Obama was working at a Chicago law firm when she met her husband and future U.S. President Barack Obama.

Her reign as first lady has been focused almost entirely on current social issues, specifically poverty, healthy living, and education for women and children. For Obama, it seems no cause is too small—even volunteering in Washington, DC–area soup kitchens and homeless shelters without pretense. Continually pushing for healthy living, Obama is a strong supporter of the organic food movement, helping schools plant gardens and putting large efforts into campaigns to end childhood obesity.

There are still many causes worth sacrificing for, *so much history yet to be made.*

Every day, the people I meet *inspire me*… Every day, they make me proud… Every day they remind me how **blessed we are** to live in the greatest nation on earth.

One of the lessons that I grew up with was to *always stay true to yourself* and never let what somebody else says distract you from your goals. And so when I hear about negative and false attacks, I really don't invest any energy in them, because *I know who I am.*

You can't make decisions based on fear and the possibility of what might happen.

You may not always have a comfortable life and you will not always be able to solve all of the world's problems at once, but don't ever underestimate the importance you can have because history has shown us that courage can be contagious and hope can take on a life of its own.

I wake up every morning in a house that was built by slaves. And I watch my daughters, two beautiful, intelligent, black young women playing with their dogs on the White House lawn… And as my daughters prepare to set out into the world, *I want a leader who is worthy of that truth*, a leader who is worthy of my girls' promise and all our kids' promise, a leader who will be guided every day by the love and hope and impossibly *big dreams that we all have for our children.*

I am an example of what is possible when girls from the very beginning of their lives are *loved* and *nurtured* by people around them. I was surrounded by extraordinary women in my life who taught me about *quiet strength* and *dignity*.

Jacqueline Kennedy Onassis

THERE ARE MANY LITTLE WAYS TO ENLARGE YOUR CHILD'S WORLD. LOVE OF BOOKS IS THE BEST OF ALL.

As one of the most popular First Ladies, Jacqueline Kennedy Onassis brought elegance to the White House through her intelligence and cultured upbringing. Like so many First Ladies, though, Kennedy Onassis was so much more than a cultured wife and mother.

After becoming First Lady in 1961, Kennedy Onassis accepted the daunting task of making the White House a home for her children, Caroline and John Jr., and Patrick, who died shortly after his birth from respiratory complications. She then turned her attention to the rest of the White House to restore its historical essence and cultural significance. Her entertaining skills were legendary, as was her social and cultural prowess, giving her a reputation for hosting magical and awe-inspiring events.

Most admire Kennedy Onassis for her strength throughout the tragedy of her husband's assassination. After the death of her second husband, Aristotle Onassis, Kennedy Onassis returned to New York to pursue an editing career. She continued her work until her untimely death in 1994. She remains a symbol of twentieth-century American fashion, poise, and grace under pressure.

I am a woman above everything else.

We should all **do something to right the wrongs** that we see and **not just complain** about them.

I'll be a *wife and mother first,*
then First Lady.

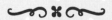

The only routine with me is
no routine at all.

Rosa Parks

I DO THE VERY BEST I
CAN TO LOOK UPON LIFE
WITH OPTIMISM AND HOPE
AND LOOKING FORWARD
TO A BETTER DAY.

Growing up in Montgomery, Alabama, Rosa Parks quickly gained firsthand experience with prejudice and inequality. For years, she lived with the knowledge that blacks in the South were not entitled to the same rights as those in the North, until she decided to take a stand.

In 1955, when Parks refused to give up her seat on a Montgomery bus to a white man, her defiance ignited a bus boycott of 381 days. Rosa Parks's action gave thousands of individuals the courage to speak out against the injustice toward southern blacks, furthering social acceptance and equality in America.

Time magazine named Parks one of the most influential and iconic figures of the twentieth century. The Rosa Parks Congressional Gold Medal bears the legend, "Mother of the Civil Rights Movement."

Each person must *live their life* as a model for others.

⌐❈⌐

Memories of our lives,

of our works, and

our deeds will

continue in others.

⌐❈⌐

Whatever my individual desires were to be free, I was not alone. There were many others *who felt the same way.*

❧ ✻ ❧

I have learned over the years that when one's mind is made up, this diminishes fear; *knowing what must be done* does away with fear.

I would like to be known as a person who is concerned about *freedom and equality* and justice and prosperity for all people.

I would like to be remembered as a person who wanted to be free...**so other people would be also free.**

Amy Poehler

GREAT PEOPLE DO THINGS
BEFORE THEY'RE READY.
THEY DO THINGS
BEFORE THEY KNOW
THEY CAN DO IT.

Amy Poehler is an American comedian, actress, director, and writer. Born near Boston, Poehler studied at Boston College before moving to Chicago to join comedy theaters Second City and ImprovOlympic. Poehler received her big break when she was a cast member of *Saturday Night Live* and has since received various awards and a star on the Hollywood Walk of Fame for her contributions in television.

Aside from her acting and comedy career, Poehler is also a humanitarian who is active on women's issues. She has cofounded the organization and website Amy Poehler's Smart Girls, which aims to help young people discover their identities. The website is devoted to encouraging and supporting girls to change the world.

When young girls are *encouraged to explore* what they find interesting, they grow up to be *interesting women.*

It's okay to not be looking at what everyone else is looking at all of the time.

No one looks stupid when
they're having fun.

Girls, if a boy says something that
isn't funny, you don't have to laugh.

I think if you can dance and be
free and not embarrassed,
you can rule the world.

I just love bossy women. I could be around them all day. To me, bossy is not a pejorative term at all. It means somebody's *passionate* and *engaged* and *ambitious* and *doesn't mind leading.*

Vulnerable people are *powerful people.* Opening your heart and sharing it means you're going to get so much love in your life.

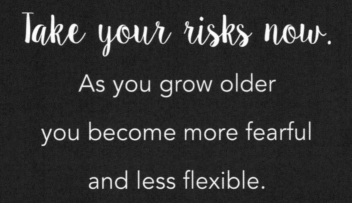

Take your risks now.

As you grow older

you become more fearful

and less flexible.

Condoleezza Rice

WE CANNOT BE
RELUCTANT TO LEAD
AND YOU CANNOT
LEAD FROM BEHIND.

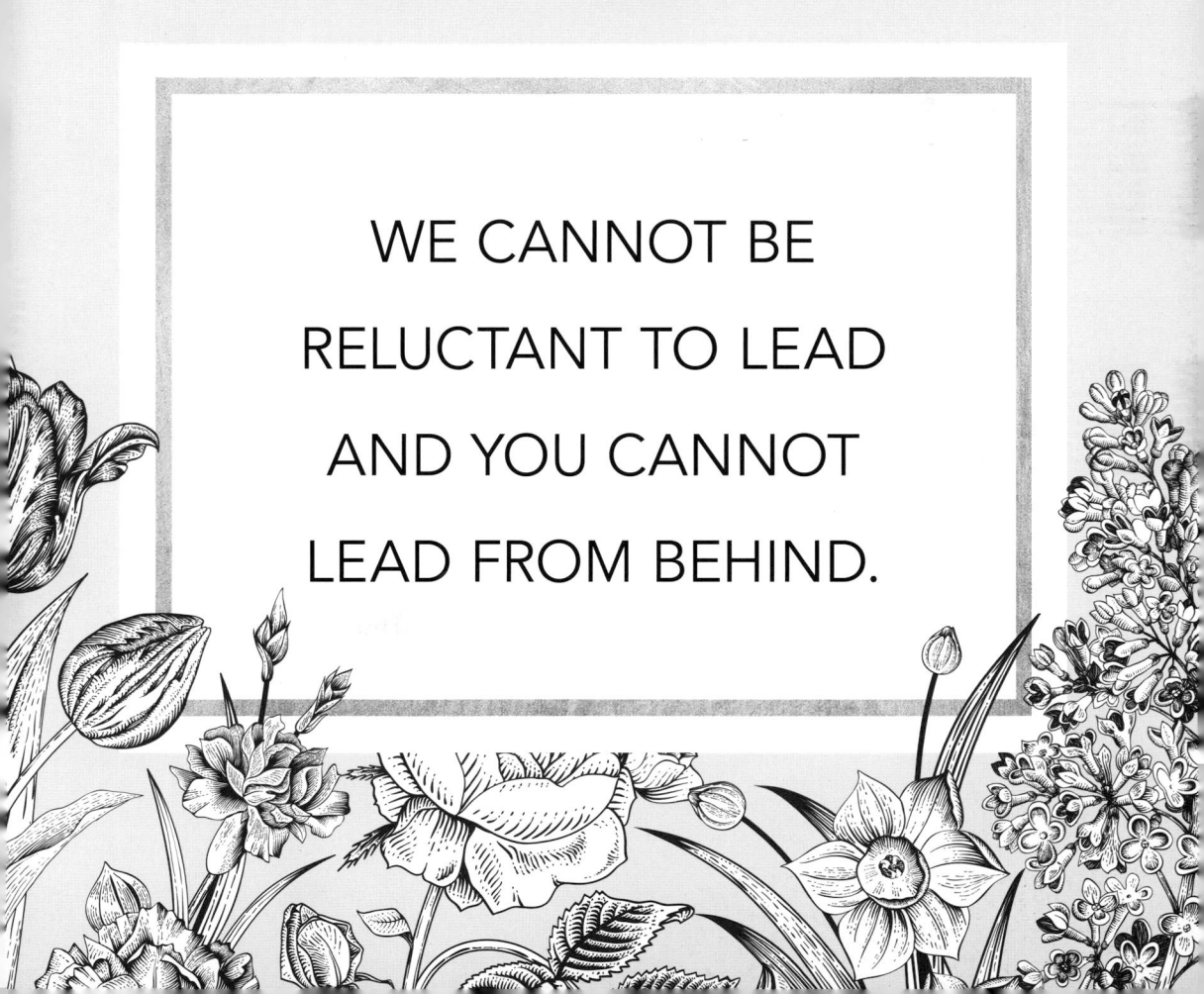

Not only is Condoleezza Rice the second woman to ever be named U.S. secretary of state, she also has the noted distinction of being the first African American woman to hold the position. Extraordinarily gifted, Rice skipped both the first and seventh grades, allowing her entrance to the University of Denver at age fifteen. Continuing her education, she earned two additional degrees, one being her PhD in international studies.

Impressed by Rice during a 1980 fellowship, Stanford University offered her a teaching position, where she remained a popular professor until her appointment to provost. In 2000, President George W. Bush appointed her national security advisor, making her the first African American and woman in the post. Four years later, Rice again made history by being named the sixty-sixth secretary of state.

With tenacity, intelligence, and determination, Condoleezza Rice continues to shatter the glass ceilings of society.

Differences can be a **strength**.

The people of the Middle East share the desire for *freedom*. We have an *opportunity*–and an *obligation*–to help them turn this desire into *reality*.

Foreign policy is ultimately about security—*about defending our people, our society, and our values*, such as freedom, tolerance, openness, and diversity.

People may oppose you, but when they realize you can hurt them, they'll join your side.

The essence of America—
that which really unites us—
is not ethnicity, or nationality
or religion—it is an idea—
and what an idea it is: That
you can come from humble
circumstances and do great
things. That it doesn't matter
where you came from but
where you are going.

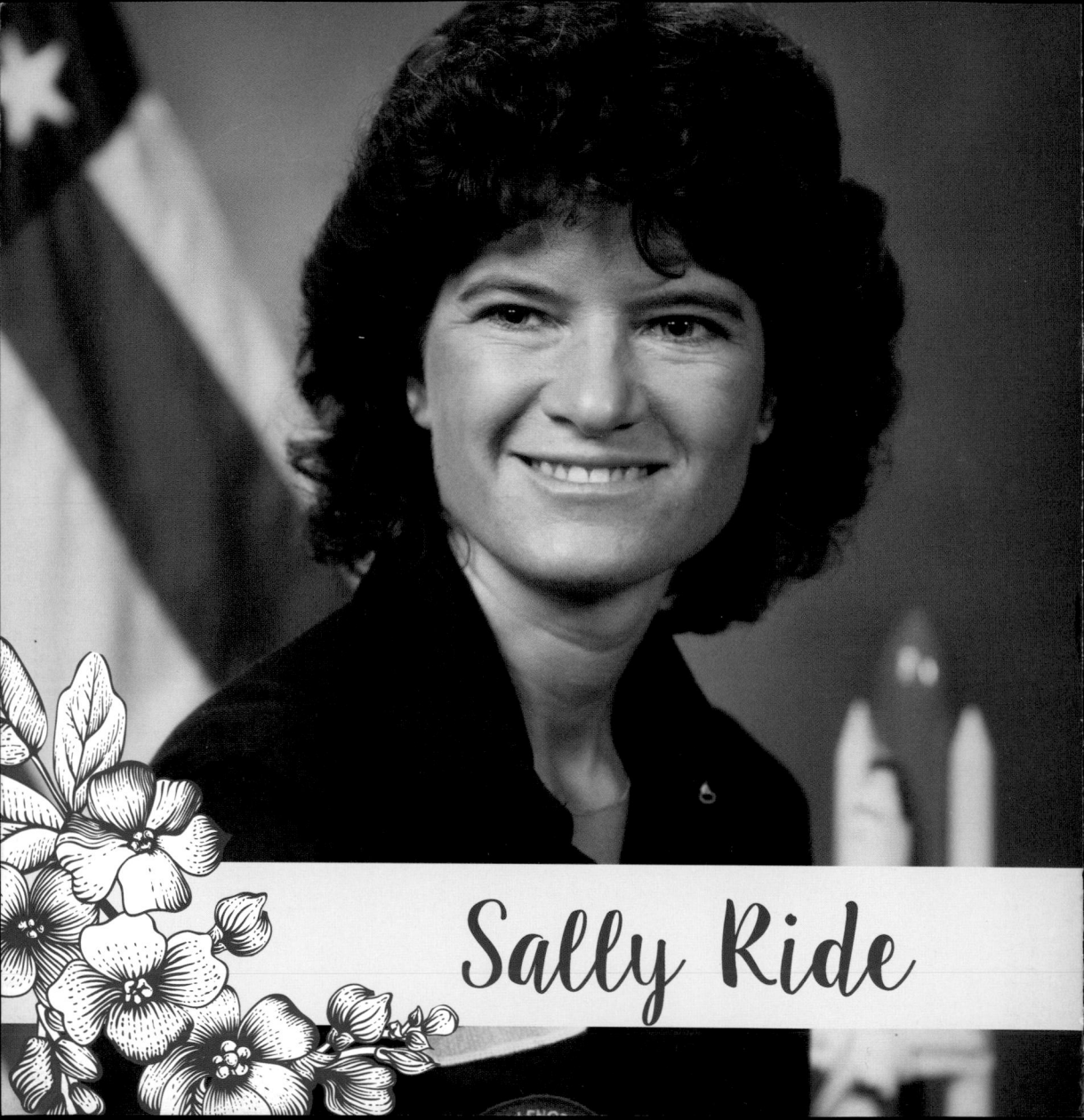

Sally Ride

I WOULD LIKE TO BE
REMEMBERED AS SOMEONE
WHO WAS NOT AFRAID TO
DO WHAT SHE WANTED
TO DO, AND AS SOMEONE
WHO TOOK RISKS ALONG
THE WAY IN ORDER TO
ACHIEVE HER GOALS.

Originally an American physicist and astronaut, Sally Ride became the first American woman in space in 1983. After growing up in Los Angeles, Ride went to Stanford University to study physics and English and stayed at the school until she had earned her PhD in 1978. That same year, Ride was accepted to the National Aeronautics and Space Administration's (NASA) astronaut program, a position for which 1,000 other applicants had applied. Ride was the third woman and the youngest American to travel to space. While at NASA, she was a part of the investigations of the *Challenger* and *Columbia* space shuttle disasters and was the only person to participate on both.

In 2001, Ride founded a company to promote educational opportunities for young girls and to encourage them to take part in science and math.

I suggest **taking the high road** and have a little sense of humor and let things roll off your back. I think that's *very important.*

The fact that I was going to be the first American woman to go into space carried huge expectations along with it. I didn't really think about it that much at the time…but I came to *appreciate what an honor it was* to be selected to be the first to get a chance to go into space.

It means a lot to me that my participation in that flight has meant so much to so many people. And I hadn't appreciated how much it did really mean to people, how much it touched *particularly women*, until after my flight. The first few months after my flight I was really struck by the way that women of all ages—from college students to sixty-year-old, seventy-year-old, eighty-year-old women—reacted to me. It was just something that they never thought they would see. And it *made quite an impression on me.*

For whatever reason, I didn't succumb to the stereotype that science wasn't for girls. *I got encouragement from my parents.* I never ran into a teacher or a counselor who told me that science was for boys.
A lot of my friends did.

Young girls need to see role models

in whatever careers they may choose,

just so they can picture themselves

doing those jobs someday.

You can't be what

you can't see.

LIFE WAS MEANT TO BE
LIVED, AND CURIOSITY
MUST BE KEPT ALIVE.
ONE MUST NEVER, FOR
WHATEVER REASON, TURN
HIS BACK ON LIFE.

Anna Eleanor Roosevelt, known to most simply as Eleanor, was a United Nations diplomat, humanitarian, and wife of President Franklin D. Roosevelt. More than that, though, Eleanor Roosevelt was one of the most widely admired women in the world and to this day continues to be an inspiration to many. In particular, she is recognized for her outspoken nature and controversial viewpoints—Roosevelt refused to stand idly by her husband when she saw a need to answer.

During her twelve years as First Lady (1933–1945), the unprecedented breadth of her activities and advocacy of liberal causes made her nearly as controversial a figure as her husband. Roosevelt instituted regular White House press conferences for female correspondents for the first time. In deference to the president's illness, she helped serve as his "eyes and ears" throughout the country. She showed particular interest in such humanitarian concerns as child welfare, slum clearance projects, and equal rights.

After President Roosevelt's death, in 1945, President Harry Truman appointed Eleanor Roosevelt a delegate to the United Nations, where, as chair of the UN Commission on Human Rights, she played a major role in the drafting and adoption of the Universal Declaration of Human Rights.

The giving of **love** is an *education* in itself.

It isn't enough to talk about peace.

One must believe in it.

And it isn't enough to believe in it.

One must work at it.

Only a man's character is the
real criterion of worth.

❧✖❧

Life was meant to be lived...
One must never, for whatever reason,
turn his back on life.

❧✖❧

What one has to do usually can be done.

When you *cease* to make a contribution, you begin to die.

I think it is a *tremendous loss* to a child to grow up in a *family without conversation.*

It is not fair to ask of others what you are not willing to do yourself.

You gain strength, courage, and confidence by every experience in which you really stop to look fear in the face... *You must do the thing you think you cannot do.*

J. K. Rowling

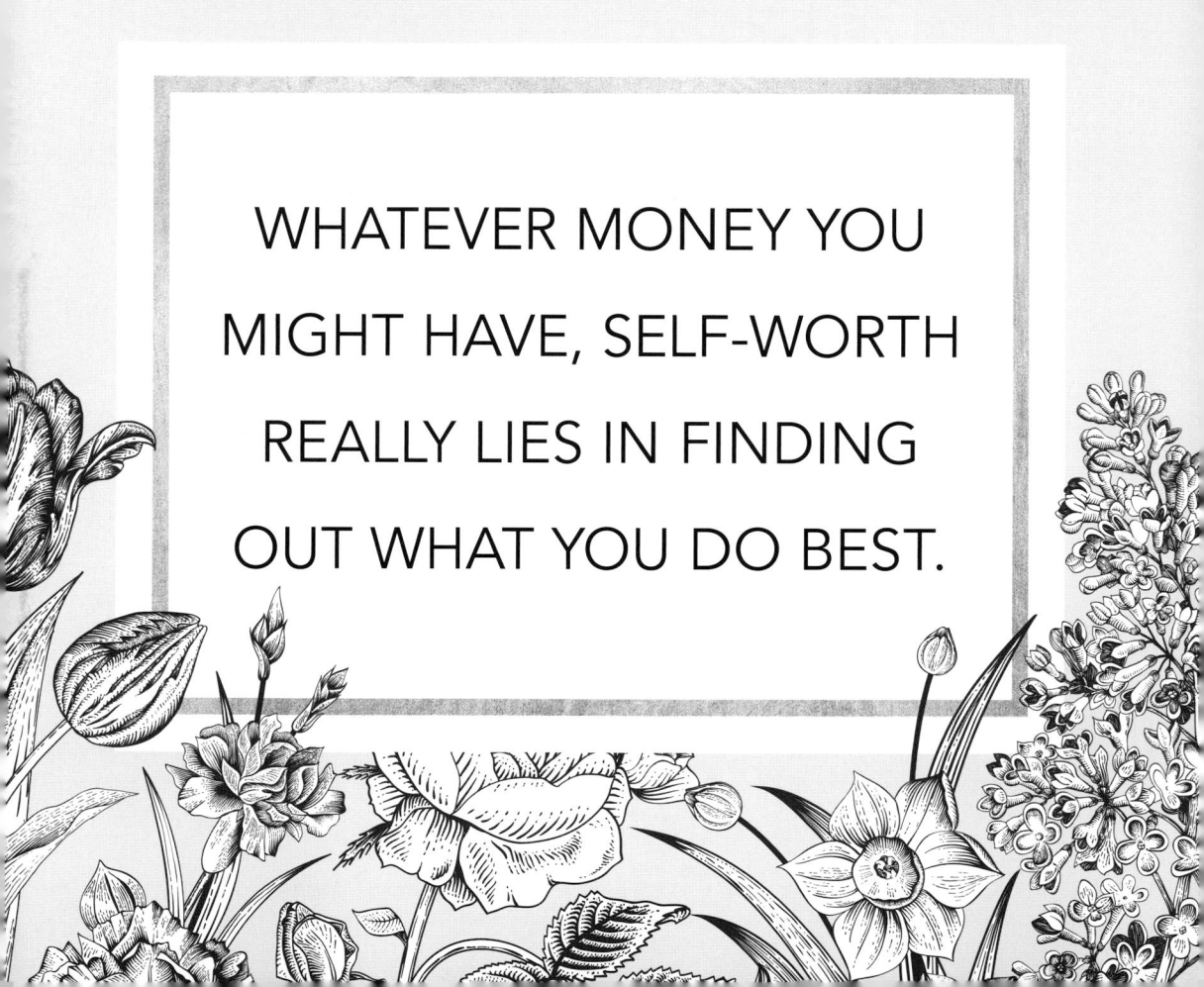

WHATEVER MONEY YOU MIGHT HAVE, SELF-WORTH REALLY LIES IN FINDING OUT WHAT YOU DO BEST.

Joanne "Jo" Rowling is a British novelist, screen-writer, and film producer best known for writing the Harry Potter series. Before writing the bestselling book series in history, Rowling was a single mother who was on the verge of poverty.

Rowling has used her fame and success to support charities like Comic Relief, One Parent Families, the Multiple Sclerosis Society of Great Britain, and Lumos. She has been called the Most Influential Woman in Britain as she gives social, moral, and political inspiration to her fans.

We do not need **magic** to
change the world, we carry
all the power we need inside
ourselves already: **we have
the power** to imagine better.

Love is the strongest power there is.

As is a tale, so is life:

not how long it is, but how good it is,

is what matters.

You might never fail on the scale I did, but some failure in *life* is *inevitable*. It is impossible to live without failing at something, unless you live so cautiously that you might as well not have lived at all—in which case, you fail by default.

You will never *truly know yourself*, or the *strength of your relationships*, until both have been tested by adversity.

What's coming will come and we'll just have to meet it when it does.

It takes a great deal of **bravery** to stand up to our enemies, but just as much to stand up to our friends.

❧✻❧

Anything's possible if you've got enough nerve.

Wilma Rudolph

NEVER UNDERESTIMATE
THE POWER OF DREAMS
AND THE INFLUENCE OF
THE HUMAN SPIRIT.

One of twenty-two children, Wilma Rudolph grew up in Tennessee. Stricken with polio at an early age, Wilma believed she would one day walk again without braces because of her mother's inspiration.

When she was nine, the braces were removed, and Rudolph spent all of her free time running and at play. In the years that followed, she was extremely active in basketball and track. She excelled as an athlete, and her years of dedication were rewarded in 1960 at the Olympic Games in Rome. Rudolph was the first woman to win three gold medals in one Olympics in track and field.

Wilma Rudolph passed on her skill and determination as the track director and special consultant on minority affairs at DePauw University. As an outstanding field and track champion, Wilma Rudolph raised women's track to the forefront in the United States.

My mother was the one who made me *work*, made me believe that one day it would be possible for me to *walk* without braces.

When the sun is shining, I can do anything; no mountain is too high, no trouble too difficult.

Sometimes it takes years to really grasp
what has happened to your life.

I would be very disappointed if I were
only remembered as a runner because
I feel that my contribution to the youth
of America has far exceeded the woman
who was the Olympic champion.
The challenge is still there.

The triumph can't be had without
the struggle.

Sheryl Sandberg

WE HOLD OURSELVES BACK
IN WAYS BOTH BIG AND
SMALL, BY LACKING SELF-
CONFIDENCE, BY NOT
RAISING OUR HANDS, AND
BY PULLING BACK WHEN WE
SHOULD BE LEANING IN.

Sheryl Sandberg is an American technology executive and activist who is the chief operating officer of Facebook and author of the bestselling book *Lean In: Women, Work, and the Will to Lead*. With a degree from Harvard Business School, Sandberg worked in government for a few years but left to take part in the booming industry of technology, particularly at Google.

Sandberg was the vice president of Global Online Sales and Operations and helped launch Google.org, which is the charitable arm of the company. With a reputation of professional success behind her, Sandberg went to work for Facebook, and in June 2012, she became the first woman to serve on Facebook's board.

As a strong activist for women's rights, Sandberg serves on the board for Women for Women International and has given a TED Talk entitled "Why We Have Too Few Women Leaders."

The **upside of painful knowledge** is so much greater than the downside of blissful ignorance.

What would you do if you weren't afraid?

Being *confident* and *believing* in

your own self-worth is necessary to

achieving your potential.

It is the ultimate luxury to combine passion and contribution. It's also a **very clear path to happiness**.

⤜✹⤛

I think when tragedy occurs, it presents a choice. You can give in to the void, the emptiness that fills your heart, your lungs, constricts your ability to think or even breathe. *Or you can try to find meaning.*

If I had to **embrace** a definition of *success*, it would be that *success* is making the **best choices** we can… and *accepting them*.

～�֍～

Knowing that things could be worse should not stop us from trying to make them better.

Trying to do it all and expecting that it all can be done exactly right is a recipe for disappointment. *Perfection is the enemy.*

⌒⚘⌒

I feel really *grateful* to the people who *encouraged* me and *helped* me develop. *Nobody can succeed on their own.*

Margaret Chase Smith

MORAL COWARDICE THAT KEEPS US FROM SPEAKING OUR MINDS IS AS DANGEROUS TO THIS COUNTRY AS IRRESPONSIBLE TALK.

Maine native Margaret Chase Smith began her political career in 1940, when at the age of thirty-three she became a member of the Republican State Committee.

In 1940, Smith was elected to the Seventy-Seventh Congress. Her work as an advocate for female status in the military while on the House Naval Affairs Committee earned her the title "Mother of the Waves." The independent-thinking congresswoman from Maine served eight years in the House of Representatives until she was elected to the U.S. Senate in 1948.

Margaret Chase Smith's honest, straightforward way gained her widespread popularity across the country and serious consideration to be America's first female vice presidential candidate.

I believe that in our constant search for security we can never gain any **peace of mind** until we are secure in **our own soul.**

Greatness is not manifested by unlimited pragmatism, which places such a *high premium* on the end justifying any *means and any methods*.

My **creed** is that public service must be more than doing a job **efficiently** and **honestly**. It must be a **complete dedication** to the people and to the nation with full recognition *that every human being* is entitled to **courtesy** and **consideration**, that constructive criticism is not only to be expected but sought, that smears are not only to be expected but fought, *that honor is to be earned but not bought.*

The right way is not always *the popular and easy way*. Standing for right when it is unpopular is a true test of **moral character**.

One of the basic causes for all the trouble in the world today is that *people talk too much and think too little*. They act too impulsively without thinking.

Meryl Streep

THE BIGGEST LESSON I LEARNED IN MY CAREER WAS TO ASK OTHER PEOPLE WHAT THEY MAKE. BECAUSE THE MEN USUALLY MAKE MORE THAN YOU DO. AND IT'S GOOD TO KNOW. YOU'RE NOT ALLOWED TO ASK. BUT IT'S GOOD TO ASK.

Known as one of the best American actresses in history, Meryl Streep uses her fame to promote gender equality. This winner of multiple Academy Awards, Golden Globes, and Tony Awards is also a spokesperson for the National Women's History Museum and argues for equal gender pay. Additionally, Streep has supported Gucci's "Chime for Change" campaign, an organization aimed at spreading empowerment and education to girls and women. Streep has also established scholarships at the University of Massachusetts and funded a screenwriters' lab for female screenwriters. On a global landscape, Streep has signed an open letter for the ONE Campaign, urging leaders in Germany and South Africa to focus on women in their development goals for the generation.

I'm sort of **in love** with what
I don't know. I'm in awe of
what is not **explainable**
or **predictable**.

You have to *embrace* getting older.
Life is precious and when you've
lost a lot of people, you realize
that *each day is a gift*.

It's good to push yourself and do what you don't necessarily want to do, that if you're not automatically good at it, you should try it. *Trying is so important.*

⌒∞✱ᴄ⌒

I want to feel my life while I'm in it.

⌒∞✱ᴄ⌒

The *great gift* of human beings is that we have the *power of empathy.*

INTEGRATE WHAT YOU BELIEVE

IN EVERY SINGLE AREA OF YOUR LIFE.

TAKE YOUR HEART TO WORK AND

ASK THE MOST AND BEST OF

EVERYBODY ELSE TOO.

People will say to me, "You've played so many strong women" and I'll say, "Have you ever said to a man, 'You've played so many strong men?'" No! Because the expectation is [men] are varied. Why can't we have that expectation about women?

Power, influence, strength—all those things can overpower what's important in life. But as long as you have food and shelter over your head, if the necessities are taken care of, what makes us happy on top of that is very simple.

Margaret Thatcher

I LOVE ARGUMENT, I LOVE DEBATE. I DON'T EXPECT ANYONE JUST TO SIT THERE AND AGREE WITH ME, THAT'S NOT THEIR JOB.

Margaret Thatcher was the first woman in European history to be elected prime minister.

The daughter of a grocer, she received her degree in chemistry at Oxford, where she became president of the University Conservative Association. During the 1950s, she worked as a research chemist and also studied law, specializing in taxation.

Thatcher ran for Parliament in 1950, but it was not until 1959 that she was finally elected to the House of Commons. She served as parliamentary secretary to the Ministry of Pensions and National Insurance and later as education minister. She was elected the leader of the Conservative

Party in 1975, and the party's victory in the 1979 elections elevated her to the office of prime minister.

Margaret Thatcher became known as the "Iron Lady" because of her dedication to the ideals in which she believed and the grace to get them accomplished.

Advisers advise, and ministers *decide*.

What is success?

I think it is a mixture of having a flair for

the thing that you are doing; knowing

that it is not enough, that you have

got to **have hard work** and a certain

sense of purpose.

I am **extraordinarily patient,**

provided I get my own way

in the end.

I've got a woman's ability to *stick to a job* and *get on with it* when everyone else walks off and leaves it.

Pennies don't fall from heaven.
They have to be earned on earth.

❧ ✹ ❧

Let our *children grow tall*, and
some taller than others if they have
it in them to do so.

Harriet Tubman

I HAD REASONED THIS OUT IN MY MIND, THERE WAS ONE OF TWO THINGS I HAD A RIGHT TO, LIBERTY AND DEATH. IF I COULD NOT HAVE ONE, I WOULD HAVE THE OTHER, FOR NO MAN SHOULD TAKE ME ALIVE.

Born a slave in Maryland, Harriet Tubman yearned to be free. In 1849, she made her escape to Pennsylvania through the Underground Railroad. She then used that route nineteen more times, returning to the South to lead more than three hundred slaves to freedom.

As the years passed, Tubman became known as the "Moses" of her people, directing them out of an enslaved land. During the Civil War, she served the Union Army as a nurse and a spy. With black soldiers, she mobilized an effort to free slaves who had not been released by their masters.

Following the war, Tubman raised funds to construct schools for ex-slaves. She labored for female suffrage and, in 1903, established a shelter for poor, homeless blacks.

An American heroine, Harriet Tubman is remembered as an extraordinary humanitarian.

I would fight for my *liberty* so long as my *strength lasted.*

Every great dream begins with a dreamer. Always remember you have within you the **strength**, the *patience*, and the **passion** to reach for the *stars to change the world.*

I grew up like a neglected weed~ ignorant of liberty, having no experience of it.

I had crossed the line of which I had so long been dreaming. *I was free*; but there was no one to welcome me to the land of freedom. *I was a stranger in a strange land.*

I freed a thousand slaves. I could have freed a thousand more if only they knew they were slaves.

When I found I had crossed that line, I looked at my hands to see if I was the same person. There was such a glory over everything; the sun came like gold through the trees, and over the fields, and I felt like I was in Heaven.

Meg Whitman

DO WHAT YOU LOVE
AND SUCCESS WILL
FOLLOW. PASSION IS
THE FUEL BEHIND A
SUCCESSFUL CAREER.

Meg Whitman is the president and CEO of Hewlett Packard Enterprise and chairwoman of HP Inc. As an American business executive, political activist, and donor, Whitman has worked for companies like DreamWorks, Hasbro, and The Walt Disney Company. She played an instrumental role in the development and success of eBay as the president and CEO of the company.

Aside from business, Whitman also has interests in politics, and in 2008, the *New York Times* considered her among the women most likely to become the first female president of the United States. Two years later, Whitman ran for governor of California but lost the election to Jerry Brown.

In an effort to give back, Whitman founded the Griffith R. Harsh IV and Margaret C. Whitman Charitable Foundation by donating 300,000 shares of eBay stock in 2006. The proceeds of this foundation are donated to help the environment and schools.

Guess *what?*
The world *changes.*

Problems are good,
as long as you solve
them quickly.

A business leader has to keep their organization focused on the mission. That sounds easy, but it can be tremendously challenging in today's competitive and ever-changing business environment. A leader also has to motivate potential partners to join.

"Perfect" is the enemy of "good enough."

Oprah Gail Winfrey

THE GREATEST DISCOVERY
OF ALL TIME IS THAT A
PERSON CAN CHANGE
HIS FUTURE BY MERELY
CHANGING HIS ATTITUDE.

Known as the Queen of All Media, Oprah Winfrey has been called the greatest Black philanthropist in American history.

Born into poverty and raised in inner-city Milwaukee, Oprah worked hard to overcome familial struggles, sexual abuse, and socioeconomic class barriers to become one of the most influential and powerful women in the world.

As a talk show host, actress, producer, and philanthropist, Oprah has shared her success to help others. In 1998, she launched Oprah's Angel Network, which provided grants to nonprofit organizations and supported charitable projects around the world. Her charity program ran for over a decade, donating money to schools and disaster relief. She has also founded the Oprah Winfrey Leadership Academy for Girls in South Africa to provide better opportunities for girls who have disadvantaged backgrounds.

I am a **woman in process**.

I'm just trying like everybody else.

I try to take every **conflict**, every

experience, and learn from it.

Life is **never dull**.

I will continue to use my voice. I believed from the beginning that [the lawsuit] was an attempt to muzzle my voice, and I come from a people who have struggled and died in order to have a voice in this country. And I refused to be muzzled.

I never think about what I want. It's about what you want to give to other people.

I was raised to believe that excellence is the best deterrent to racism or sexism. And that's how I operate my life.

I believe that everyone is the *keeper of a dream* and by tuning in to one another's secret hopes, we can become better friends, better partners, better parents, and better lovers.

So go ahead. Fall down.
The world looks different from the ground.

❦

My philosophy is that not only are you responsible for your life, but doing the best at this moment puts you in the best place for the next moment.

❦

Be thankful for what you have; you'll end up having more. If you concentrate on what you don't have, you will never, ever have enough.

Challenges are gifts that force us to search for a new center of gravity. **Don't fight them.** Just find a different way to stand.

⤬

The reason I've been able to be so financially successful is my focus has never, ever for one minute been money.

⤬

You know you are on the *road to success* if you would do your job, and not be paid for it.

Susan Wojcicki

THOUGH WE DO NEED MORE WOMEN TO GRADUATE WITH TECHNICAL DEGREES, I ALWAYS LIKE TO REMIND WOMEN THAT YOU DON'T NEED TO HAVE SCIENCE OR TECHNOLOGY DEGREES TO BUILD A CAREER IN TECH.

Known as the Most Important Person in Advertising, Susan Wojcicki is the CEO of YouTube. With degrees in history and literature from Harvard University, Wojcicki originally planned on pursuing a career in academia with a PhD in economics; however, her plans changed when she developed more of an interest in technology.

Having worked in marketing at Intel, Wojcicki left to become Google's first marketing manager in 1999. As the vice president of advertising and commerce, Wojcicki helped develop Google Images, Google Books, and AdSense (which became the second largest source of revenue at Google). She also oversaw Google Video and had proposed to the company's board that they should purchase YouTube. She handled this acquisition for the company and became the CEO of YouTube in 2014.

Work **smart**.

Get things done.

No nonsense.

Move fast.

Things are always changing. Part of being successful here is being comfortable with not knowing what's going to happen.

Life doesn't always present you with the perfect opportunity at the perfect time. Opportunities come when you least expect them, or when you're not ready for them. Rarely are opportunities presented to you in the perfect way, in a nice little box with a yellow bow on top... Opportunities, the good ones, they're messy and confusing and hard to recognize. They're risky. They challenge you.

From phones to cars to medicine, technology touches every part of our lives. If you can create technology, you can change the world.

Malala Yousafzai

I RAISE UP MY VOICE NOT SO I CAN SHOUT, BUT SO THAT THOSE WITHOUT A VOICE CAN BE HEARD. WE CANNOT SUCCEED WHEN HALF OF US ARE HELD BACK.

Malala Yousafzai is a Pakistani activist for female education and the youngest-ever Nobel Prize laureate. She grew up in the Swat Valley and when the Taliban started attacking schools for girls, she began speaking out for women's rights at the age of eleven. Four years later, Yousafzai was targeted by the Taliban and shot in the head. She survived the attack and returned to her activism stronger than before.

In 2014, Yousafzai received the Nobel Peace Prize, and in 2015 she opened a school for Syrian refugee girls in Lebanon.

When the whole world is *silent*, even one voice becomes *powerful*.

Even if I am a girl,

even if people think I can't do it,

I should not lose hope.

We were scared, but our fear *was not as strong as our courage.*

❧ ❊ ❧

I don't want to be thought of as *"The girl who was shot by the Taliban"* but *"The girl who fought for education."* This is the cause to which I want to devote my life.

Let us make our future now, and let us make our dreams tomorrow's reality. What is interesting is the power and the impact of social media… So we must try to use social media in a good way.

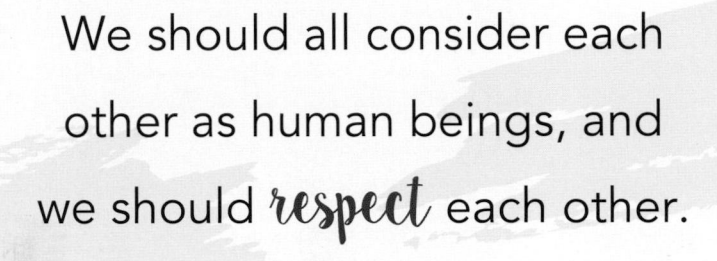

We should all consider each other as human beings, and we should *respect* each other.

The **best way** to solve **problems** and to fight against war is *through dialogue.*

Photo Credits
Cover: front, Olga_Korneeva/Thinkstock, letoosen/Thinkstock; back, June Letters Studio
Internals: page 1, June Letters Studio; page 2, Olga_Korneeva/Thinkstock; page 6, Olga_Korneeva/Thinkstock, Christiane Amanpour/Speakerpedia; page 10, Olga_Korneeva/Thinkstock, June Letters Studio; page 12, Chris Felver/Getty Images, Olga_Korneeva/Thinkstock; page 18, June Letters Studio; page 20, PhotoQues/Gettty Images; page 26, Hulton Deutsch/Getty Images; page 34, George Rinhart/Getty Images; page 42, Steve Granitz/Getty Images; page 48, Jason Merritt/Getty Images; page 56, Robert Gray/Getty Images; page 64, Ron Galella/Getty Images; page 72, Mireya Acierto/Getty Images; page 78, GraphicaArtis/Getty Images; page 86, Chip Somodevilla/Getty Images; page 92, Bettmann/Getty Images; page 98, Bettmann/Getty Images; page 106, Adam Berry/Getty Images; page 112, Bettmann/Gettty Images; page 118, Paul Morigi/Getty Images; page 128, Michael Ochs Archives / Stringer/Getty Images; page 134, William Philpott/Getty Images; page 142, s_bukley/Shutterstock; page 150, Rob Kim/Getty Images; page 158 Time Life Pictures/Getty Images; page 166, Hulton Archive/Getty Images; page 174, Cindy Ord/Getty Images; page 182, Bettmann/Getty Images; page 196, Mark Kauffma/Getty Images; page 204, Jaguar PS/Shutterstock; page 212, Keystone/Getty Images; page 220, MPI/Getty Images; page 228, Deborah Feingold/Getty Images; page 234, Jaguar PS/Shutterstock; page 242, Jason Merritt/Getty Images; page 248, da Mae Astute/Getty Images

Published by Simple Truths, an imprint of Sourcebooks, Inc.
P.O. Box 4410, Naperville, Illinois 60567-4410
(630) 961-3900
Fax: (630) 961-2168
www.sourcebooks.com

Printed and bound in China.

PP 10 9 8 7 6